Is
Yucatan Peninsula, Mexico

Mexico

written and researched by
E.A. Farro

Athyrium guides make good reads. They are written by professional writers and artists to provide you with authentic details of the cities and neighborhoods you want to explore.

Copyright © 2017 Athyrium Travel

ISBN 978-0-9992096-0-8

Contents

Introduction

Isla Holbox is a small island in the Yucatan Peninsula north of Cancun. Most of the island is protected wilderness, but there is a lively small town on the western toe. There are no cars and no big resorts, making this an ideal destination for those looking for a break from the hustle and bustle of modern life - but not too much of a break as cell phone service and internet access are readily available. The island food is a main attraction. Restaurants range from traditional Mexican to more European influence with multiple thin crust pizza places, French bakeries, and Italian gelato. Visitors include everyone from couples on romantic vacations to families with small children to backpackers traveling alone.

Why I wrote this guide: I visited the island on a whim. I had found enough online to be intrigued, but not enough in guides to know what to expect. I fell in love immediately. Thrilled with my experience, I realized how inadequate traditional guides can be for small places.

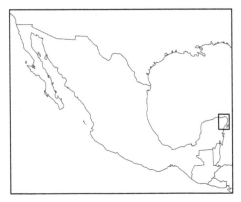

How to read this guide: The guide can be used as a reference, skipping around to sections as needed, or it can be read cover to cover. A travel essay gives the reader a sense of place, which is usually so lacking in traditional guides. Sections on eating out and hotels provide recommendations for a range of travelers. Businesses were included based on my experience and research. No one provided payment or incentive to be in the guide. The hand drawn map orients the reader by sunrise and sunset viewing and shows the places discussed in the book.

How to get there: A twenty minute ferry through calm waters from the town of Chiquilá. The closest airport to Chiquilá is Cancun. You have three options from Cancun:
- Rental car: You can pay to park at the ferry dock. The drive is under two hours.
- Taxi: Arrange ahead through hotels or private companies. The drive is under two hours.
- Bus: One leaves midday from the central Cancun station. The ride is four to five hours.

Buying this book supports the local community: One of the island charms is the dog population. The health of the dogs is supported by voluntary veterinarians. That is why ten percent of the book proceeds will go to the Isla Holbox Spay Neuter Project to help maintain their services. Healthy animal populations protect human communities too.

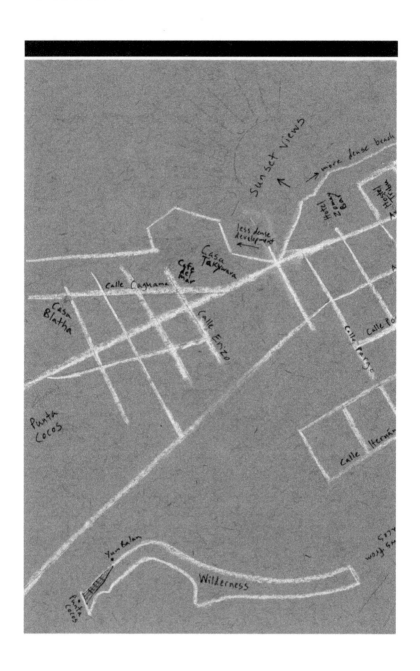

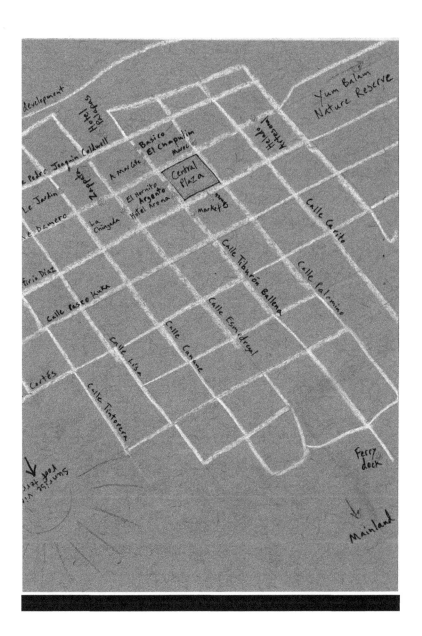

In the Moment

A travel essay that gives a sense of place on Isla Holbox

The distinction between indoors and outdoors is unclear, and shoes are optional in either. The streets are paved with sand, as are the floors of shops and cafés. There are no cars, no chain stores, no big resorts. We use walkie-talkies like cell phones, the range excellent without large buildings to block the signal. Many cafés don't have four walls, a floor, and a ceiling, but some subset of these. There are outdoor kitchens and bars without walls. Waterfront views for drinking, eating, and sleeping are ubiquitous. The characteristic island architecture is palapas – open walled huts with thatched roofs made of dried palm leaves lashed to a wood frame. Inside, I look up and admire the exposed wood beams that can reach cathedral heights.

It's a few days before Christmas 2016, and after weeks of declining daylight and the increasing cold and rain at home, I'm desperate for open space and sunlight. I need a break from my 9-to-5 job and 24/7 phone. My husband and I started our careers as field scientists and never lost the craving for wilderness and open space. The logistics of going totally off grid with our sons, who are about to turn four and seven, is too much. I've settled for a vacation niche of islands. Even better, islands without traffic lights.

The trip to Isla Holbox is easy even with small children and without speaking Spanish - a direct flight to Cancun and a two-hour taxi ride that we set up ahead through our hotel to the small town of Chiquilá. We sit on the outdoor deck of the ferry for a twenty-minute ride across the lagoon with rhythms and melodies from another passenger's boombox that makes us all sway and nod and feel that we are in a movie with a soundtrack. Golf-cart-taxis wait at the ferry dock to take passengers to the center of town (walkable with a backpack instead of a suitcase).

It's a barrier island, which means it's nothing but sugary sand. There is no rock beneath, no anchor. The water is shallow; I can never walk out far enough to get above waist high. The beaches are ideal for small children. Over thousands of years, the island will migrate as waves move the sand. This can also happen in an instant – a big enough hurricane will destroy the town and reshape the island. In 2005, Hurricane Wilma caused so much damage it took businesses several months to reopen. Things are built for today; this is a place for living in the moment.

The island is shaped like a hockey stick, and just the toe at the west end is developed. The town has a central plaza a few blocks from the beach. The beach extends west and east of the center of town. To the west, sand is kept in place by twenty-meter long groins, which look more like arms than their namesake. These give an industrial aura that is mixed with a heavy dose of festivity from the hotel cabanas, beach bars, and open-air restaurants. To the east, the beach opens and a sandbar runs parallel to shore. This is more the postcard vision of undeveloped beauty. Just past the last hotel, the **Yum Balam Nature Reserve** marks the end of commerce – *Yum Balam* is Mayan for *Lord Jaguar*. This is the start of mangrove-lined beaches. On land they support endangered wild cats (… Lord Jaguar is not an exaggeration), and in the water they support whale sharks and dolphins (summer season tourist attraction!). The reserve is also home to many birds, including flamingos and migrating birds that come from as far as the arctic. Most exploration takes place from the water (by foot on the sandbar or by boat on a tour), as the forest is thick with bugs and larger wildlife.

It's a ten-minute taxi ride from the ferry to **Casa Blatha**, our hotel, or rather the hotel we *think* we are staying. We start on the busy sand-paved streets of town, but soon turn onto the beach, driving past open palapas that provide shade to beach goers. We check in at a beautiful three-story building with a screened in sand-floored restaurant and a courtyard with hammocks. The owners give us homemade popsicles and tell us someone is sewing new curtains that will be ready shortly. From the rooftop terrace I see the woman sewing under a tree in the yard.

Despite a warm welcome, we don't stay long. New construction has popped up three feet from the door of our room; a barbed wire fence and a construction crew fill our beach vista. The hotel owner shrugs and says someone else owns that land, and they are building a beach bar. Power tools roar at us and we leave on friendly terms, promising to come back for lunch another day. We cross our fingers and head out on foot. A five-minute walk towards town, we see a big palapa with two canvas tents and a few hammocks slung between palm trees. This is **Glamping**, glamorous camping. The tents have gorgeous blue tiled showers, a narrow entryway with a bench for shoes, and an air-conditioned bedroom that fits a full bed and a small shelf. We sign up for the night, but learn A/C can't remove humidity in a tent, and that there is something like a rave on the other side of the palm trees from us.

We get lucky on our third attempt. In the center of town we stay at the crisp yellow **Hotel Arena.** Here we quickly find our groove. We take full advantage of the rooftop bar and small pool. The ambient noise of town is joyful and not disturbing. I delight over the bright colored plant holders that line the stairwell up from the street - two-liter plastic soda bottles turned on their sides and cut open, painted blue or red or green, and overflowing with spiky aloe leaves. We don't know it yet, but here at the central plaza we will be at the epicenter

Palapa on the beach

of Christmas on Holbox.

Much of what I see on the island would be labeled back home as: DIY, pop-ups, locally made, found objects, reclaimed, bike delivered, solar powered. The unique beauty of handmade and human powered is not an intentional choice here so much as the reality of an island in a developing country where building your own, recycling, and composting are a necessity. Hipster life without irony. Each object and building is touched by personal expression, a humanity that my manufactured furniture and office building lack.

I trace tree rings on my table at **Café del Mar**, the table is a varnished slice of an enormous tree trunk. I am reminded that there is so much I have not thought of, have not seen. This is the reason I travel – to be reminded that the world is enormous and I am small. An Italian waitress brings out homemade bread and fresh squeezed juice. I ask her about the table and together we study the years of drought, rainstorms, and fires preserved in the concentric circles.

On the walk back to town I stop at the open garage doors of a wood shop next to the **Hostel Tribu**. Tools glint in the sun while a worker smokes on the stoop with a sleeping dog at his feet. I ask what he makes, and he responds as if it were obvious, "Tables, chairs, and any other furniture the hostel needs."

The sense of freedom here starts with the lack of cars, being able to walk and bike in the streets and on the beach. I rent an adult tricycle and my seven-year-old rides in the basket, my husband rents a girls bike with a child seat that our four year old rides in. Between outdoor café seating, potholes, sleeping dogs, families on foot or smashed onto a single motorcycle, staying "in your lane" doesn't make sense like it does at home. Streets are malleable public spaces. While there are stop signs, red with the word ALTO, no one stops at them. The pace is slow enough and there are so many other moments that force stopping. Directions are often given in English, "turn left and then left and then right," but this is meaningless without clear landmarks. We use the murals on the sides of houses and buildings to guide us. As cafés and street vendors pop up and disappear throughout the day and week, it is hard to pin down locations. While Google Maps shows street names, there are no street signs and no one refers to the streets by name. But the stretches of street with commerce off the central plaza are short, and rambling is part of being on Isla Holbox.

The island dogs – clean and groomed – wander freely: a Great Dane at the corner store, a Pug running down the beach with a Collie, Dalmatians sleeping under a bar stool, Terriers eating trash, Chihuahuas in the lap of motorcyclists, mutts racing the sun set. The island has an animal clinic where you can visit and volunteer to take dogs on walks (and see the raccoon that lives there). My four-year old jumps into my lap or climbs me like a tree when we see a dog, but my seven-year old kneels down and puts out his hand to see if they will approach. When I was seven I plotted to have at least ten dogs when I grew up, but like many dreams this has not been practical. We don't have any pets. So with my youngest perched on my shoulders, I kneel with my oldest and we laugh together as dogs lick us and look into our eyes. I am reminded of a depth in myself that transcends verbal communication. By greeting so many dogs, I pay more attention to the dance of body language between my boys and me. I see that more is expressed racing down a beach with them than just the footprints we leave in the sand.

Island visitors include people traveling for several months, wanderers who don't plan to return home, and then the rest of us who are here to break our usual routine. We are here for a week. The quality of dreads and tattoos is notable. I chase a handsome gay male couple to ask about a forearm tattoo - it was drawn from a photocopied cedar branch. Backpackers regularly walk up the main drag from the ferry alone and then converge with others in the central plaza. I imagine their bags filled with worn cloths and journals oscillating between lonely reflection and wild stories. Families are everywhere, pushing strollers, kids running ahead, the occasional kid driving a golf cart. We meet a Venezuelan who lives in Ottawa, many business owners and tourists from Mexico City, and other travelers: British, Germans, Russians, Italians, Spanish, French, Norwegians, and Moroccans. While we have no trouble getting around with English, the majority of tourists speak Spanish. Most of the Americans I meet are European expatriates.

We don't just meet people once; we make friends. The openness is what I imagine the first day of college would feel like without nerves. I strike up conversation on the beach with a couple from New York, and the next day we run into them in town and they take us to their favorite lunch spot. We hear our names shouted midday

Beach west of the town center

A worker's bike and a palapa construction site

when we are getting smoothies and turn to see Russian beach friends waving goodbye as they ride to the ferry in a golf cart with suitcases on their laps. Only on an island could a social fabric instantly spring into place.

Our British friends ask us to meet them at the plaza in the evening. This will be our introduction to a Mexican tradition. There is a night carnival in the central plaza with people of all ages. It is like a County Fair, but it happens every weekend and nightly over the holidays. There are stands with games - I shoot an air gun at targets that make skeletons dance and sing. There are rides - my boys ride chipped airplanes and motorcycles around and around a tree with *Winnie the Pooh*. The streets are lined with vendors selling tortas, tacos, corn, and churros. The heat and humidity lift, breathing energy into the town.

While the island is full of people passing through, there is a sense of safety. Local women tell me that they walk alone at night. I forget my backpack in my bike basket parked along the beach overnight – it has my camera and some money in it. When I remember the next morning, the bag is there and no one has touched it. At the beach, we leave our bags and toys on the sand and go into the water. We never have much on us, but always a few things that would be easy for a thief to grab. They don't.

The shadow side to this freedom comes as wafts of burning trash early in the morning, a fallen structure, like an abandoned games of Pick-Up-Sticks, between fancy beach hotels, a spa with a pile of trash next to its grand front door. It is as if each establishment feels that it stands on its own. But without regulation, everyone's investments are at the mercy of each other. Glamorous camping sites can't advertise quiet if there is a rave next door, and beachfront hotel rooms will fail if someone else can own and build on the last stretch of sand before the water.

When I ask about building regulations, I am told, "This is the Wild West." It is freedom from oversight. No one is suffocated here by building codes; no one is limited by zoning. But that means when my kids race up the stairs ahead of me to a rooftop terrace, my stomach falls to my feet when I see there is no railing. It means that while I can walk up stairs with a limp rope hung as a banister, my Grandma couldn't. In the collective, regulations protect us and anticipate what we cannot of our own vulnerabilities.

We still have not formulated a Christmas plan, but we aren't worried. On the morning of the twenty-fourth we bike eastward to the sand bar, nap midday, and then head for drinks on the beach. We run into our British friends and together walk into town to find dinner. Some restaurants are closed; everything open is packed. We sit outside a small café without a sign just off the plaza. The owner takes our order; he is Parisian. After our beers come, giant raindrops splatter the table. We run in and stand looking around at the giant TVs with soccer and all the full seats. The owner waves a hand at us, as if to say, *no worries*. He sets up a table in the kitchen and we settle in to eat grilled lobster and steak. Two Dachshunds run under our table making the kids yell with surprise and the rest of us laugh. After, we go to the plaza and let the kids jump in the bounce house.

I'm just thinking it's time to take the children inside when sirens blare. A police truck drives into sight; Santa Claus rides on the back. Children run to form a group behind the truck and grab at candies Santa is throwing. I chase after my boys who run without looking back. My feet are swollen with humidity from the day. At night, in the air conditioning, they will return to their normal size. The truck circles the plaza, stopping at the town hall. Santa calls names over a loud speaker and children dressed in frills and smart shirts run up to get their presents. The children take their new toys into the plaza. A dad runs holding up a young girl on a bike; a boy tries his roller skates out on the stage; a mom tries to get her toddler to sit on a tricycle. Storefronts host parties that spill far into the street with TVs and chairs and children in party dresses.

After helping my husband herd our children back to the hotel, I sneak out. I had seen a sign for a "Rooster Mass" at 10 p.m., but only a few people are sitting in the church when I arrive. Outside, families and children shriek and play. I sit and study the white stucco arches for twenty minutes and then go outside and watch the crowd. Just as I'm about to give up, the bell rings. Everyone, from the youngest to the oldest, files inside. A ceiling fan moves the hot air and I regret my long sleeves. Candles flicker on stage around a nativity scene. A simple Jesus hangs at the center of the altar. A man plays guitar and three women sing Spanish songs into microphones, the congregation sings along. I don't understand the words, but the feel and sound are life affirming. Whether the sign was wrong or the priest decided to start an hour late, I don't know, but it is another reminder to let go of the rigidity I carry in my daily routines.

I go back to my hotel to sleep, the festivities continue, giving way to clubbing music. It's still going when I wake. I pull on a sweater and go to the roof balcony to watch the sun rise. A new song comes on; there is yelling, and the song changes. The church bell rings at 7:45 a.m., the music goes silent. A crowd gathers and goes inside.

Christmas Day we stop in front of a hostel to watch a man open a coconut with a machete. He is grilling lobster with a group of young twenty somethings. They let our kids drink from the coconut and then offer us a sip mixed with rum and ice. The twenty-somethings list off their countries, each from somewhere far away and different than the others. I'm drawn in by their laughter and my own curiosity, but my boys pull at me to go. The island has its own current, bringing us together with strangers to tell our stories then pulling us apart to continue on our way. We haven't needed any plans; we just jump into the current and see what happens.

I relish the absence of cars, predictable chain stores, and work. I came to get away, but finding freedom is as much an internal as an external experience. The lack of routine is a start, but it is the discovery of something new each day that actually transforms us – a friend, a café, a flamingo, the feel of riding a bike under the stars on a beach. It is the experience of wonder that reminds me of myself.

I snuggle my youngest son in the hammock chair that hangs off the bar, my feet grazing the soft beach sand. He tells me that the pink and orange in the sky is food coloring. I sip my passion fruit margarita and feel the embers of holiday spirit inside me. I know they will keep me warm through the rest of the winter.

Near the town center

Dining

We eat everything. From fine dining to street food, our meals are delicious: fresh squeezed juice, homemade pasta, grilled shrimp, brick oven empanadas, fresh croissants, gelato, mezcal blended with fresh mango, tequila blended with fresh cucumber and mint. Generally, at a sit down restaurant, our family of four ate for $50 U.S. at the high end ($$$), and around $15 U.S. at the low end ($). The food options reflect the native Mayans and the diversity of transplants from Europe, Africa, and other parts of Mexico.

We buy tamales wrapped in banana leaves with tiny beans embedded in the cornmeal dough. A petite Mayan woman in a traditional embroidered dress sells them from a cart she pushes through the streets. We eat *marquesitas*, a rolled up crepe that cools to a brittle crisp and is filled with shredded cheese. We buy fresh squeezed juice at the market: *jugo rojo* (beet and orange), *jugo naranja* (carrot and orange), and *jugo verdé* (chaya, pineapple, orange). Chaya is an herb like basil with a less distinct flavor. In addition to jugo verdé, it's in omelets, pestos, and dipping sauce at pizza joints. It's a native Mayan plant that irritates the skin raw; but cooked has extensive health benefits.

It's not safe to drink water from the tap. Treated water and ice are brought by ferry, delivered by bike, carried up stairs by a young man wearing a yoke. The value of water is recognized. Restaurants often serve flavored water - cantaloupe, cucumber, or a blood red hibiscus. We bring our own water bottles and buy large jugs of water at corner stores to refill them. We have a backpacking filtration pump, but never bother to use it.

Even the children are impressed by the options for sweets. We decide to hunt for dessert and find too many

choices in the center of town: **Maroc** or **A Mar Café** for fresh coffee and homemade cake, **Helado Artesanal** for gelato, or street vendors selling churros and marquesitas. We choose Maroc where the barista is from Italy and the owners from Morocco; both fell in love with the island on visits and never left. On my son's fourth birthday we get chocolate lava cake from the just opened and very fancy, *Basico*. Our British friends have sentimental recipes made for them at A Mar Café for Christmas.

You can look up restaurants, some are anchor points, but things change fast. Places appear and disappear throughout the day and week. When a restaurant closes for the day or for a break in the day, they lean a sheet of plywood against the front door, or hang orange tape like it is a construction zone. A few hours later it might be open again. This makes every visit feel like a new discovery.

More Restaurants:

La Chingada $ - A sidewalk lunch café with an outdoor kitchen on the front of an apartment building. La Chingada is the crass nickname for the indigenous lover and translator of Hernán Cortés, the Spanish Conquistador who conquered the Aztec empire. Telling someone to go to chingada means *go to hell*. The café specializes in ceviche - seafood cooked with citrus (versus cooked with heat), fried fish, and tacos. Beer is available. It's frequented by both locals and tourists. The owners, a middle-aged couple, talk to costumers as they mix blends of fresh lime and roasted habanero (the roasting process makes it tingle with spice, but not burn). A mural of bright yellow, green, and pink fish throbs across the narrow road and serves as a landmark.

Le Jardin $$ – A bakery with a line out front. They make croissants, tomato tarts, muffins, baguettes, and egg dishes. You can call ahead to make a reservation for large groups (many Mexican tourists do this). They open at 8:30 a.m. and can sell out quickly. I bought the last chocolate croissant at 9:30.

Casa Blatha $ - For foodies and botanists, the owner will walk you through the garden and show you the plants they use in their tea, smoothies, and omelets. They were only open for breakfast while we were there. The restaurant is screened in and has a sand floor. They make their own juice, popsicles, pesto, tortillas, jam, and bread. If you stay here, I recommend the main building, which is surrounded by a garden that provides a buffer to construction and the road. Keep children away from the roof terrace, it has no rail.

Zappata $$$ - The bar at the front has a mix of stools and swings. Cocktail makings are on display: cinnamon sticks, herbs, celery, cherries, agave leaves. The dining area has a sand floor. At night the restaurant is packed, and the grill is lit. The grilled platter for 2 could serve 6 or maybe even 10 with fresh lobster, crab, shrimp, octopus, fish, and mussels served with salsa and lime. Watching all the action is fascinating. Some of the wait

An open air restaurant

staff are barefoot, others wear sneakers. There is live music. Children join each other to play at a small table with toys, speaking in a cacophony of different languages. On the cheesy end of the spectrum, the food is not exquisite, but it was one of our most memorable nights.

El Hornito Agrento $$ – Across from the plaza, this wood grilled pizza place has prime outdoor seating for people watching. The pizzas are good; the wood-fired empanadas with chaya dipping sauce are amazing.

El Chapulim $$$ – Close to the plaza and open only for dinner, this posh restaurant is beautiful. The chef comes out to tell you about the menu - they offer a small number of choices each night. We had fresh fish on a bed of zucchini in butter with oregano, a side of potatoes cooked in dill, and something between a salsa and a slaw with zucchini, mango, cucumber in a citrus sauce with herbs. None of it was spicy; all of it was flavorful. They only take cash.

DON'T DO THIS: We had heard that we should bring all the cash we would need, but at the airport we didn't feel like figuring out what that meant. When we got to the island, we saw ATMs, lulling us into thinking we didn't need to worry about access to cash. Near the end of our trip, out to dinner at a very nice restaurant we realized we only had a few small bills left. We had already ordered. I ran out to an ATM thinking I would be back before the food came. The first ATM was out of service. I darted across the central plaza to a second ATM, it was out of cash. Sweating by then, I criss-crossed the plaza to a third ATM, an ominous message popped up and no money came out. I called my bank with the help of a hotel on the plaza to confirm nothing was wrong with my account (by now I was spinning all kinds of horror stories). I ran back to the restaurant and tried to put the gorgeous food into my churning stomach. Full of shame, I told the owner I did not have money to pay. The owner was gentle with me, which made me feel even worse. The next morning the ATM that had been out of cash was replenished and willing to hand over some bills. I then paid my dinner bill.

Fresh cocktails at Zomay, Hotel Arena, Basico (left to right)

Accommodations

Accommodations range from tents to cabanas to fancy hotels with pools. Surge pricing happens at peak times, like Christmas. Staying on the beach gives direct access to fresh air and an ocean view. Staying in town is convenient for checking into a home base before going out. Hotels are popping up everywhere. I recommend making a reservation ahead, but read recent reviews before you go. When you arrive, check out the place before paying. If you aren't happy, look online (internet is everywhere) or just walk along the beach and through town to find a place. It was easy for us to relocate when we hit a snag at our first hotel. At off peak times, it would be okay to show up with no reservations. A taxi driver in a golf cart will show you places. After exploring numerous hotels and talking to others about their experiences I came up with the recommended list below.

Hotel Arena $ – Across from the main plaza in the center of town, this is extremely convenient and economical. The rooms are simple and clean. There is a rooftop deck with a great view and proper rails. By day, a cooling off pool is open, easily mistakable for a hot tub. By night, the bar serves some of the freshest blended cocktails. An ideal spot to view sunrise or sunset. The front desk is friendly and helpful.

Casa Takywara $$ – The gorgeous grounds, main building with rooms, and cabana on the beach are a ten-minute walk from the center of town. This is one of the nicest areas of beach with a wide sandy area clearly separated from the lane where bikes and golf carts drive down the beach.

Hotel Arena

Hotel La Palapa $$$– This posh hotel is notable for making fresh pasta and not allowing children. It's on the beach in a dense line up of hotels, just off the center of town. I stuck my tongue out at the manager when he asked if the small boy I was holding hands with was my son because, "children are not welcome." I'm jealous of travelers that can transcend the chaos of children, and this is a lovely hotel in which to do that.

Hostel Tribu $ – In the center of town and just off the beach, the complex includes a bar, communal kitchen, a courtyard with swings and hammocks, and yoga classes. There are single rooms, double rooms, and dorm style rooms with bunk beds. This is the least expensive way to stay on the island, and a great way to meet other people. They host activities including, salsa dancing, BBQs, pub quizzes, and jam sessions. This is a loud place oriented to those interested in socializing and nightlife. They discourage children staying there, but were happy to let my kids explore the beautiful grounds.

DON'T DO THIS: We arrived tired and ready to run and jump in the water, so we paid for the whole week upfront. It turned out that since I made the reservation, ownership had changed hands and a construction project had begun very close to the property. The place was not going to work out - I was able to get my money back and move on. But not every hotel is that nice. Before you pay, check out the room and hotel and make sure you are comfortable.

Rooftop view of town

Itineraries

Itineraries

Morning #1
Breakfast at → Punto Cocos → Look for
Casa Blatha   Beach   starfish

Morning #2
Breakfast at → Pick up fresh juice → Look for
Le Jardin   at the central market   flamingos

Afternoon and Evening
Sunset cocktails → Dinner at → Central Plaza ⬈ Salsa dancing
at Zomay   El Chapulim   Carnival   ⬊ Rooftop bar

Morning notes: *Wait to go out until the sun comes up to avoid mosquitoes. Many stores and restaurants opened between 7 and 8 a.m. If you are a runner, the beach is excellent for long runs. Morning is a great time to be active before the heat of the day.*

Morning Itinerary #1

Bike or taxi to **Punta Cocos,** the beach at the very western toe of the island. There are no shops or vendors at the beach so bring drinks and snacks along with you. A nice stop on the way for breakfast is **Casa Blatha**. Ask the owner to show you around the garden. When you get to Punta Cocos, head straight for the water. The trees and plants on the beach house mosquitoes, but once you are ankle deep in water you will be safe. The water is extremely shallow and calm. Walk and look for white, red, and brown starfish. We only found them at this beach. If you took a taxi here, walk back to town along the beach - there will be no taxis to hitch rides back. It will take an hour or more to walk back along the beach.

Morning Itinerary #2

Stop by **Le Jardin** for croissants - they run out so get there at or before they open at 8:30 a.m. and be prepared to wait in line a few minutes. Stop by the **market** in the plaza for fresh squeezed juice. The bottles are easy to pack and take with you. Bike, walk, or taxi east out of town where the road widens and runs along the beach. You can stop anywhere you like or go to the end where there is a nature reserve (the road turns right after **Villas Tiburon By The Beach** and runs behind the hotels). Wade out to the sand bar - bring juice, water, snacks, and sand toys. You can settle in and relax, walk, or explore the shallow water. Look for rays (one foot wing span, they look like a dinner napkin folded in half), flamingos (they tend to be by the river delta), and egrets. Head to town and stop at **La Chingada** near the center for ceviche and beer. Talk to the owner, the other costumers, and watch the beautiful dogs wander by.

Mid day and Night time notes: Midday can be hot and humid. We always showered off the morning sand and sunblock, ate, and rested. The city wakes up after dark. The central plaza is busy and full of locals as well as tourist. Off of the center, the streets and the beach can be very dark. We used headlamps for walking or biking. Taxis were available from the center of town.

Afternoon and Evening Itinerary:

Go to the **Hotel Zomay Bar** on the beach. The bar is a small palapa. Sit in swings at the bar and watch drinks being made with fresh fruit, or sit at a table on the sand with dogs sleeping under your chair. My favorite was the passion fruit margarita, the kids' favorite were the mango smoothies. Watch the sunset and have a drink. BEFORE the sun has set all the way, go inside to avoid mosquitoes. You will also beat the dinner rush. Go to **El Chapulim** for a splurge. After dinner, head to the plaza for the nightly carnival, snack on sweets from the street vendors and test your luck at a few games. Then head to **Hostel Tribu** for salsa lessons or the **Hotel Arena** balcony for cocktails.

Packing List

<u>Essentials</u>

Sun protection: Sunglasses, hats, sunblock. You can buy sunblock on the island.

Bug protection: Light-weight long-sleeves and bug spray. You can buy bug spray on the island.

Flashlight: For areas off the main plaza at night.

Warm clothing: An extra layer for cool mornings.

Cash: Many places take credit cards, but many do not. There are a few ATMs on the island, some for U.S. dollars and some for Pesos. Sometimes the ATMs don't have money or are broken. Don't rely on ATMs; bring the cash you need. We took money out at an ATM at the airport and kept cash in money belts on our bodies when we were in transit. At our hotels, we used safes or asked the owners to hold our passports and cash. We exchanged some U.S. dollars at the smoothie place, Angeles Y Diablitos, across from the main plaza.

<u>We Enjoyed Having</u>

Headlamps: We used these for hands free walking and biking at night.

Walkie talkies: Cell phones work on the island, but we like to disconnect from home. Our cheap walkie talkies worked as a way to keep in touch with each other through the day.

Art Supplies: Sketch pad and pencils to draw.

Running clothes: The beach is perfect for running in the mornings.

Reusable water bottles: We refilled bottles with store bought gallons of clean water.

Packing List

Swim suits
~~Backpacking water filter (check it still works)~~ didn't use
Head lamp
walkie Talkie
T-shirts
Shorts
Dresses
2 books
Notebook + pens
Old phones for camera
~~Fancy camera~~ didn't use
~~Running stuff~~ never ran
Sandals
Sun glasses
hats
~~Rain gear~~ didn't rain
~~Fanny pack~~ forgot to use
~~Hammock~~ They were all over already
Sun block
lotion
lip balm
Shampoo + conditioner
Hair gel
Water bottles

TO DO

* Taxi reservation
- Set timer at house
- Mail xmas gifts
- Call credit card co.
- Find money belt
- Pack passport!!

E.A. Farro is a P.h.D. scientist and a writer. Her works include the series, Science Love Letters, as well as essays and stories published in places like Rumpus, The Normal School, and Kenyon Review.

Send your thoughts and stories to her about Isla Holbox to farro.scribe@gmail.com.

CPSIA information can be obtained
at www.ICGtesting.com
Printed in the USA
BVHW060034010421
603811BV00002B/151